Elevate
TO EXPAND

MICHELLE P COREY

BALBOA.PRESS
A DIVISION OF HAY HOUSE

Balboa Press books may be ordered through booksellers or by contacting:

Balboa Press
A Division of Hay House
1663 Liberty Drive
Bloomington, IN 47403
www.balboapress.com
844-682-1282

Print information available on the last page.

ISBN: 979-8-7652-4602-3 (sc)
ISBN: 979-8-7652-4601-6 (e)

Library of Congress Control Number: 2023919140

Balboa Press rev. date: 10/20/2023

Contents

Acknowledgements

To my beautiful souls that I have had the gift of bringing up, my first born John and my precious Nicole. You have opened my heart more than you know. My hope is that you have better awareness and insight than I did at a younger age.

To my grandchildren: My Carina, you awakened my spirit when you were born. Your pure soul still amazes me. James, I love how you know who you are and what you want. You teach me. Shane, your gentle soul and kindness is what we all should strive for. Lance, your determination is to be admired. May you all become your full potential and use every gift God gave you.

To my dear soul friends that I have the opportunity to grow my soul with, Rose and Barbara. I thank you for our daily chats and encouragement. You have been there for me and I appreciate you.

To Rick, for believing in me, and being a major part in my soul journey.

God gave me the honor of having you all in my core soul family, and I am so grateful.

Introduction

Do you know that you can feel better at 70 than you did at 40? This is what happened to me. There is a lot you can do to improve your wellbeing no matter what your age is. Become a master of yourself and health. Good nutrition carries us far, but our complete wellness requires more than great nutrition. We are more than this.

I am headed into my seventh decade shortly, and I have never felt better physically and emotionally. This book shares with you how I got here. These steps will help you understand how to get on a path to your optimal condition no matter where you are starting.

I have not always felt awesome. Twice in my life, I had a major fall of health. Once in my mid-twenties, due to a toxic build up, and again in my late-fifties. In my twenties, I was diagnosed with rheumatoid arthritis, and I refused to accept it. This started my awareness of what pollutes the body. I recovered completely by eliminating the cause and relying on alternative modalities.

The second time made me aware that no matter how great your nutrition is, there are other factors that can knock you down. I had too many emotional hits in a short period of time. I now look at life like this. It is not what happens TO you, but what happens FOR you to evolve.

In my field of alternative medicine and biofeedback therapy, I have been fortunate to work with several functional medicine doctors and learn from them about our physical health. This, along with meeting many gifted healers and learning about energy, has helped me to know about the wholeness of ourselves. Our vitality involves all aspects of our body, mind and spirit.

I do not take for granted the blessing it is to sleep well, breathe easily, and feel wonderful throughout the day! Let's feel better every decade.

> Come learn how a lifestyle can get you to
> your optimal human potential!

Be well,
Michelle

Step One

Avoid and Eliminate the Violations
Everyday toxins create lifelong problems.

Step One is to educate yourself on all the potential hazards in your daily life, and then avoid and replace as many as possible. Let me say first off: Toxins, undernourishment, and stress are the <u>three most damaging factors</u> in premature aging! You may feel somewhat better if you start taking vitamins, but you will never feel awesome unless you remove the buildup of toxins.

Here is why:

- Our bodies are evidence of our environment as our genes respond to an overload of chemicals.
- Physiological stress produces chemicals that are harmful to the body and also block the uptake of essential nutrition.

Epigenetic researchers suggest that the majority of people's medical problems come from harmful environmental factors that force our good genes to behave badly. So at any point in life, healthy genes can start to get sick. **We must lighten**

the toxic burden. Everyone has a toxic burden, consisting of their total accumulation of Xenobiotics. The toxins the body accumulates can include anything from heavy metals to mold or parasites. If you eat lots of conventional vegetables, and you do not wash off the pesticides, you probably have an accumulation of glyphosates. This toxicity can take decades to accumulate, but it might seem to occur suddenly, as a new exposure can tip the scale.

Basically, when the burden reaches a level that exceeds the power of the detoxification mechanisms' ability to cope, a breakdown occurs. Disease usually starts with the inability to detox. When our bodies are functioning and eliminating well, we are usually disease-free.

As we age, our organs become less efficient naturally, so the burdens are even more difficult to eliminate. If you do not detoxify and cleanse regularly, you cannot nourish. Work on *detox* first, then *absorption*, *nutrients*, and *mental attitudes*.

Start to *eliminate* all low-frequency violations of the body and mind.

Organs and Systems

There is no magic pill. First, stop adding to the toxic burden. Removing violations relieves inflammation and assists the organs in detoxifying, so that is the first critical step.

Toxins do accumulate and burden our detox organs, and they are an avoidable stress. To detoxify, you need clean water, a good liver, and good kidneys.

Five organs along with two complete systems are what keep us performing at maximum efficiency. When these organs and systems become burdened with toxic overload and get congested, we begin to have health issues.

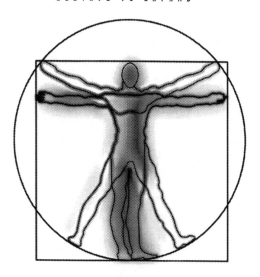

Our Five Detox Organs

Liver: One of many jobs assigned to this organ is the regulation of most chemicals in the blood and the excretion of bile. Bile helps to carry out waste. If the whites of your eyes are not crystal white, your liver is most likely congested.[1.1]

Kidneys: Your kidneys are the body's filters. They filter about ½ cup of blood every hour to remove waste and extra fluid, reduce acidic ph, and balance minerals.[1.2]

Lungs: The main function of your lungs is to help oxygen enter your red blood cells. We expel carbonic acid from the lungs. Breathe deeply.

Low Oxygen = Low Energy

Skin: Our largest detox organ is our skin, and when it is blocked with fragrant lotions, the rest of the body gets burdened. The condition of your skin on the outside shows what goes on inside.

Colon: Think of the colon as your plumbing to process and remove waste. It reabsorbs water, electrolytes, and remaining nutrients before excretion. A clean colon in good bacterial balance usually provides good health. Disease often originates in the colon. Change the bacteria, and your health will improve.

Cleansing Systems

The two systems that help the body cleanse are the circulatory and lymphatic systems.

Carrying too many toxins is the #1 factor in having a sluggish lymphatic system. The nodes and vessels are supposed to carry the toxic fluids and waste away from the cells. When they are congested, the result can be a lower immune, fluid retention, and fatty deposits. It can also be a root cause of respiratory problems and sinus infections. Dry brushing stimulates the lymphocytes as does walking, stretching, and exercising. Any way you can keep the body moving is beneficial.

The circulatory system is responsible for circulating oxygen, removing carbon dioxide, and sending waste products to the excretory organs for removal. Negative habits like having a sedentary lifestyle or consuming processed foods can contribute to lowered oxygen.

IT IS VITAL TO ADDRESS DETOXIFICATION!

First eliminate and remove, then add High Frequency ways.

Everything has a measurable frequency, measured in megahertz (MHz). The human body has a vibrational frequency of about 68 MHz. The brain is up to 90 MHz. When our cells are at high hertz, we are operating healthy. Likewise, when we are fighting a cold, our hertz drops to about 58.

High frequency ways elevate your wellbeing. However, it does not make much sense to add HF if you are negating the effort by polluting your body. The following are insights into everyday low frequency items that are worth eliminating. Each category below deserves greater attention, but I will just highlight some of the common culprits. Many of the common violations one must be aware of include: food, water, air, personal products, fragrance, technology, EMF radiation, VOCs, toxic people, and thoughts.

I am not going to focus on the biggest culprits here, but more on the unsuspecting daily violations. Remember the biggest ones are excess alcohol and sugar.

Food Toxins

Too often we consume negative nutrients, meaning food devoid of vitamins. Not only are you consuming empty calories, you are using up your reserve energy to digest it. The body compromises its own Life Force to digest negative nutrients.

Undernourishment is one of the primary causes of Premature Aging and Fatigue. You can eat regularly throughout the day but still be undernourished if you are not making positive food choices.

We have known for years that processed white flour and sugary products do not benefit health. Today's processed foods have an additional issue: If that label does not say Non-GMO, then that processed flour and sugar is lab-created through a process called bioengineering. These aren't natural, nourishing foods.

Dr. Steven Gundry says, "if it is in a box, it's not food."

> – Eat real food!

Here are some lists of common foods and ingredients that are harmful to good health. **Caution:** In addition to choosing your meals wisely, be careful of how you cook them. Avoid non-stick teflon cookware that releases harmful gasses when heated. A microwave does not enhance any nutrients and is really not the best choice.

Everyday Toxic Foods to Watch Out For:

Processed Industrial Seed Oils: These cause inflammation more than any other food. If you only eliminate one thing from reading this guide, this is it! Silent inflammation is being recognized as the underlying cause of all major diseases. This means avoiding fried foods, especially at restaurants because usually they use 'vegetable oils'. That means soy, corn, or canola – and yes, GMO – so it is not in the category of real food.

Packaged Foods: Get rid of any foods that come in a box, can, or plastic container, especially if it says bioengineered food on the package. They are not considered real food.

Tainted Olive Oils are common. Reports show many oils are not 100% olive oil. They are cut and mixed with cheaper oils like canola and sunflower, which are inflammatory seed oils, and then colored with chlorophyll. Olives are a fruit, not a seed, and can become rancid after two years. Know the source.

Animals raised on grain can disturb the gut just as much as if you ate GMO corn and soy. Note that the packaging might say "fed a 100% vegetarian diet." This meat is difficult to digest, and remember, you eat what they ate. Rely on grass-fed and humanely cared for animals.

White Table Salt is chemically cleaned. All salts are not equal. Celtic sea salt, himalayan, or Redmond real salt from Utah are full of needed minerals. Dr. Mary Jane has written an in-depth article you might reference for more information on this topic.[1.3]

Peanuts: Non-organic peanuts are one of the most heavily chemical-treated foods in the world. They can also contain an abundance of pesticides and mold. Actually a legume and not a nut, peanuts are known to disturb the digestive system.

Coffee: 91% of coffees sold today are contaminated with molds. Know your source.

Margarine and other Synthetic Foods: Synthetic fats usually contain highly-processed inflammatory Omega-6 seed oils.

Aspartame: Abundant in diet sodas and sugar-free desserts, you may not realize that aspartame can act as a neurotoxin.[1.4]

Food Coloring: Studies show eliminating artificial dyes (ex: red 40, yellow 5, and yellow 4) and preservatives (ex: sodium benzoate) significantly reduces hyperactivity in ADHD.[1.5]

Natural Flavors: This vague label could refer to 1 of 100 ingredients, but usually means MSG - an excitotoxin often disguised as *natural flavor*.[1.6] Yes, it is hard to believe!

Microwave popcorn: When microwaved, popcorn bags release a chemical that causes negative health effects, including cancer and lung conditions. It is not something you want to eat every night.[1.7]

Ingredients That Inflame Your Toxic Burden

The items below will give you reason to stop and think about what you may be consuming every day. These are some of the worst substances adding to your toxic burden.

Pesticides / Plyphosates / AKA Roundup

This well-known insecticide has been at the center of numerous lawsuits. Cereal, oatmeal, and granola bars usually have glyphosates unless you purchase organic. According to the WHO, 43 of 45 oat-based products tested positive for Round Up. Refer to the EWG Guide [1.8] for details on which popular breakfast foods were tested.

Preservatives

Did you know some preservatives cause respiratory distress? If you eat out and shortly afterwards experience shortness of breath, chances are you had either sodium benzoate, benzoic acid, or sulfur dioxide. These preservatives are one of the biggest reasons why boxed nonfoods lower your life force.

GMOs

Genetically Modified Organism crops are designed to tolerate and survive glyphosate pesticides so that only the weeds die. Those against GMOs cite scientific research that says GMOs cause allergies, infertility, reproductive problems, organ damage, insulin regulation problems, accelerated aging, immune problems, and changes to the gastrointestinal system.

Do you really want to be eating these foods? The body does not know how to process these non-foods. And unless your product says non-GMO, you can assume it contains genetically modified organisms.

Common GMO foods (USA):

- Canola oil
- Wheat
- Soy
- Corn
- Cottonseed
- Sugar beets
- Farm raised fish

In my experience working with many children that have ADD and ADHD, when we remove GMO foods, colors, and preservatives, their focus improves greatly. The same benefit may translate to adults as well.

Water

- clean water, clean body-

A home purifier and filtration system works great to remove most harmful heavy metals. In today's world, the one thing that cannot be removed with any filter is radiation. Notice how many 5G receptors are actually attached to the top of water supplies now. It's mind boggling.

Drinking water from plastic bottles all the time has its own problems. Plastic leaches chemicals into the water.

Let's not forget about parasites. Spring water can bring unwanted friends that stay a lifetime. Another reason to cleanse on a regular basis. An overload of parasites is the beginning of many problems. Some prefer house water with a really good filter system over spring water for this reason – just check the Ph and make sure it is not too acidic.

Possible toxins in unfiltered tap water:

- Heavy metals
- Lead
- Radon
- Aluminum
- Cadmium
- Mercury
- Fluoride
- Chlorine

Check the EWG database to find out what could be in the water in your location.[1.9]

Air Toxins

Oftentimes, we forget to consider the toxins that enter our bodies through the air. Air particles enter through your eyes, noise, and mouth and then travel through your lungs, which have a direct route to your blood supply. Germs and molds can make us sick fairly immediately, while we might be exposed to other air pollutants for years before we realize the toxic burden we have inhaled. Indoor sick buildings are responsible for lifelong health problems.

What to do?

First, get a home air purifier and see what the filter collects every few months. You will be shocked to see what is in your air! Cleansing the air in your home is important. Oxygen is fuel and low oxygen reduces energy. Breathing clean air will raise your energy.

Common Air Pollutants:

- Smog
- Smoke
- Heavy Metals/ Chemtrails
- Asbestos/ Insulation
- Dust
- Mold Spores
- Fragrance can contain over 1,800 chemicals. I cannot begin to express how toxic this is in your environment.

Home and Office Environment Toxins

Fragrance

What do you smell when you enter a space? If it smells nice, do you ever stop to think about the chemicals you might be inhaling? In maintaining our homes and office spaces, we use so many scented chemicals that can overload our senses.

One of the biggest sources of airborne toxins in our homes is hiding in the laundry room. **Laundry detergent toxicity** is a big unknown for most people. The fragrance is so overpowering; you cannot wash it out. If you have any respiratory issues or asthma, this can trigger you. If your energy is low, maybe your lungs are burdened with these chemicals and interfering with oxygen absorption.

Common Hazards:

- Pet sprays
- Room sprays
- Wall plug-ins
- Auto hanging chemical fragrances
- Candles
- Room sticks in a perfumed chemical liquid

Toxic Cleaning Supplies

Toxic products affect the skin and lungs. At the very least, open a window and avoid breathing the fumes when using:

- Furniture polish
- Ammonia based products
- Oven cleaners
- Carpet cleaners
- Toilet bowl cleaner

VOCS - Volatile Organic Compounds in Your Home

Chemical gasses emitted into the air can trigger breathing issues, asthma, headaches and impaired memory. The greater the quantity, and the longer the exposure, the more severe the symptoms may become. Below I have compiled a list of some of the big VOC contributors in the average home. Be cautious in choosing your home materials, decor, and furnishings. Research the ingredients and their potential effect.

- Carpet containing formaldehyde (New carpets can off-gas for years; buy wool.)
- Vinyl flooring (off-gassing)
- Hardwood floors (Toluene affects lung function)
- Composite wood products: furniture, decks
- Dry cleaning
- Paints / Adhesives/ Varnish
- Moth repellents
- New cars
- Foam
- New upholstery
- Fireplaces / Wood stoves
- Cooking unventilated
- Air Fresheners
- Flame retardant materials

Personal Care Product Toxins

Remember, any lotion or topical product that has fragrance will contain chemicals. And it soaks right into your skin. Again, your skin is a detox organ and is supposed to help you release toxins, so using toxic products works against you. Parabens and petroleum are still used in so many skin care items, including some of the luxury creams. Formaldehyde and toluene are in most nail polishes. Cosmetics have very little FDA regulation, and many leading brands still use lead in lipstick and petroleum in luxury creams. The laws have not been updated since 1938. Known carcinogen offenders such as formaldehyde and phytates are still allowed in your beauty products. Buy clean products.

Download the EWG Skin Deep App from The Environmental Working Group. You can scan a product to see the rating as to how toxic it is.

Common personal care hazards:

- Body washes [fragrance]
- Cosmetics [some brands still use lead in lipstick and tar in mascara]
- Perfume [fragrance could refer to one of 1,800 different chemicals]
- Hand soap [fragrance]
- Lotion [fragrance]
- Hair spray [fragrance sprayed into lungs]
- Deodorant with aluminum [High amounts of aluminum are found in the brains of Alzheimer patients.]
- Shampoo [fragrance]
- Hair dyes

Harmful EMF-Electromagnetic Frequencies

Too much technology!

Unseen currents can affect your health greatly. These low frequencies can interfere with your electrical activity, muscles, sleep cycles, biological processes, and nervous system. Symptoms of prolonged exposure may include anything from headache or nausea to fatigue, anxiety, or insomnia. Some people report such discomfort from EMF Radiation that they develop depression and/or self-harm fantasies.

5G transmitters are now everywhere. They have been attached to our water towers and emit radiation into our water sources as well. I do not know of a filter that will remove this.

Your best defense is to avoid exposure as much as possible.

Common WI-FI Disturbances:

- Cell phones
- Computers
- Headphones
- Any wireless electronics, like printers etc.
- Home security systems
- WiFi watches

People As Toxins - Human Parasites

Yes, people can be toxic. Have you noticed yourself feeling tired as you've walked away from someone, or just after having a conversation on the phone? Sometimes people drain us through energetic transference.

I know it is difficult, particularly with family members, but we can care for ourselves and limit the time spent around people who exhibit a toxic effect. Remember, kindness is a High Frequency.

I am not referring to the effects of helping someone that is having difficulty; I am referring to distancing yourself from those that have decided to live in chronic victimhood.

Limit or avoid time with these negative emotions:

- Complainers
- Depression
- Gossip
- Criticizing
- Negativity
- Jealousy
- Resentment

- Regret
- Hatred
- Major disfunction

More low frequency violations to consider:

- The News
- Lack of rest / sleep
- Excessive work
- Drugs
- Excess alcohol
- Unnecessary medication
- Cigarettes
- Clutter - It is energetic debris (details in Step 5).
- Fear - Creates holes in your aura and is held in the kidneys
- Anger - Eastern philosophy believes anger is held in the liver.

Toxic Stress

REDUCE STRESS - especially long term. Stress triggers your fight or flight response. When in a dangerous situation, there are evolutionary benefits to this reaction. However, when daily chronic stress triggers this response, it puts great strain on your body systems. Prolonged stress increases your risk of high blood pressure. It elevates inflammation and might even lead to artery damage. Stress also contributes to sleep disorders, which in turn can cause or exacerbate psychological distress.

A relaxed body allows the Life force energy to flow freely, and moving energy helps to restore health.

Thoughts As Toxins

Constant, emotionally low thoughts can create chronic stress, anxiety, and sleep disturbances. Toxic thoughts can also sabotage your self-image and your motivation to make good, healthy choices for yourself.

Persistent negative thoughts or false beliefs can burn your adrenals along with your energy. Try to shift the thought, and visualize a bright light over any worries.

Living Free of Toxic Burden

Become aware of ANY low vibrations; notice what is taking your energy and eliminate or reduce the exposure.

I did not fully discuss the obvious toxic habits of smoking and alcohol consumption. Instead, I've focused on the toxins that might be hidden in your life.

I know this seems like we cannot live unchallenged, but you can not only live healthy, you can thrive! Take one thing at a time. Reduce it and replace it.

Small changes matter. I would start with the laundry detergent and the bad oils. And get away from the WIFI, especially when you sleep. Charge the phone in another room.

The other Four Steps will give you dozens of ways to replace the toxins with healthier options and help you to live up to your greatest human potential.

Step Two

Cleanse and Repair

How to Manage Your Gut

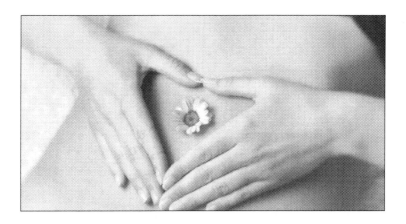

Now that you have removed the violations to the body with Step One, inflammation will begin to calm down, and the body can start to repair itself.

Note: Before you begin a cleanse, and especially a detox, make sure to nutrify your body.

Cleansing VS Detox

Cleanses are primarily focused on digestion and are short term. You can cleanse anytime. For long-term maintenance, one liquid day a week is ideal. Personally, on my liquid day I like to puree vegetables that I have simmered in homemade grass fed broth. I have learned that my body needs nutrition, but you could just have water and lemon if you choose.

The goal is to give your digestion a break. This allows your body to use your energy to heal other areas instead of digesting food. I usually have great energy the next few days. There is power in cleansing. Try this weekly for a month or two before you consider a full detox.

How to Start Cleansing

Try short cleanses for several months before you think about a deeper detox program. I have seen clients get very sick for a long time, because they started with a heavy metal detox cleanse. That is the last cleanse you would do. There is an order. First, we heal the gut and open the detox channels. Next we rid the parasites. This is not a 'more is better' model. Done responsibly, a comprehensive body cleanse or detox may take a year to complete before you can just do maintenance cleansing.

Start slowly, and try one liquid meal a day a few times. Notice how it feels and in what ways your body reacts. If you are storing accumulated toxins, they can be released too quickly, and the toxic load may be too much for your detox organs. When this happens, you will feel unwell. This is due to toxins recirculating and not moving out. Once you are able to have a liquid meal without reacting negatively, then you can graduate to having a liquid day.

Below are the recommendations I learned when visiting a wonderful cleansing detox spa.[2.1] This is the one-day cleanse that I have done successfully for years.

A Liquid Day

Simply have a nourishing liquid every hour and a half. As previously mentioned, if you choose, you can have just clean water or lemon water. I happen to be a fast burner and need more nourishment, so I opt for two meals of puree soups.

Liquids can include any of these nutrient dense options:

- Any mineral-rich broth
- Vegetable or fruit juices*
- Herbal teas
- Lemon water
- Puree soups
- Smoothies
- Chlorophyll and a glass of water
- Digestive enzymes with water
- Liquid with binders
- Liquid with fiber

I usually have lemon water tea with a little maple syrup* for the first half of the day. Then I have two meals of puree soups using my homemade collagen rich bone broth as a base. I have been doing this one day a week for years now, and it has elevated my health to a level greater than what I could have expected.

Note: Make sure you move your bowels on a cleanse day, especially if you are taking a parasite protocol at the same time.

If you need help to accomplish this, try different bowel mover herbs or an enema. You see, when you cleanse, you have die-off debris that needs to move out and not recirculate.

*Check with your physician and make sure your sugar regulation is under control, especially if you choose fruit juices or add maple syrup.

Ready To Detox?

A detox is a long term process that converts the toxins into waste and eliminates them through your detox pathways. In order to detox, it is advisable to make sure the body's detox pathways are open and not congested. A detox should be supervised, and only begun after you know how your body reacts after a simple cleanse day.

If you have negative effects from a light detox, this means your pathways and organs are too congested to handle what is being released. This is why we take specific binder supplements that grab the die-off, and make sure the detox pathways are open.

If you are unwell and want to detox, I would consult a professional.

Why Do We Need to Detox?

The body's natural detoxification system is designed to eliminate toxins as they happen. Today's exposure to daily toxins is at an all-time high. When the organs become congested, and do not work efficiently, toxins accumulate. A detox pulls toxins from the organs and restores you on a deep cellular level.

Remember, your detox organs are the liver, kidneys, lungs, skin, and colon. Your lymphatic and circulatory systems are essential to detoxification.

If you have developed body aches, headaches, or digestive issues (just to name a few), this is often because some organ is congested and not running efficiently and some form of detoxification may be necessary to feel well again. Personally, I do not believe you can heal without frequent maintenance cleansing – at least once a month. It allows the body to restore balance.

IT All Starts with the Gut!

The gut has everything to do with keeping the nervous system balanced. The Vagus Nerve connects from the brain to the gut. It is the director of the parasympathetic nervous system, also known as the 'rest and digest' system. Intermittent fasting is powerful in resetting and improving the vagal tone.

The body can heal when it is resting, free from the taxing fight or flight response.

Rules of the Stomach

1. Chew well and eat slowly, try to ensure meals are relaxed and calm. This helps stimulate the necessary enzymes that break down and assimilate food.
2. Do not eat between meals. This allows the body to build up more enzyme reserves and helps regulate your sugar metabolism.
3. Avoid drinking lots of water while eating. This dilutes the HCL in your stomach, which in turn slows the breaking down and processing of food. Drink your water between meals.
4. Eat fruit before noon. If fruit is entwined with heavy protein later in the day, it can become putrid.

Word of Caution: Remember, there is an order!

First we address parasites, then digestion, kidney, liver, and lastly heavy metals. Make sure your elimination channels are open before you start on any cleanse. I have had clients come to me very sick because they have started heavy metal chelation therapy without opening the detox channels first. This is reckless.

You cannot begin with a heavy metal cleanse; start with a parasite cleanse first, but only AFTER you open the pathways. The kidney and liver pathways need to be open or you could reabsorb the toxins and add to the toxic burden. Binders are critical when detoxing to capture and remove the toxins. Do not cleanse without binders.

Before beginning the process, see a good Functional Medicine Doctor or Naturopath, especially if you are unwell.

If you have had digestive issues for a while, consider getting parasitology testing. I have found many people have parasites and do not know it. It can be the source of many symptoms that you think are poor digestion. This is a first cleanse you should start with: a gentle parasite cleanse. Critters can clog your organs, valves, and pathways – so a parasite cleanse is always a first cleanse. If you immediately do not feel well, it is a sign your kidney and liver detox channels are not open. You may temporarily feel worse as the toxins release due to die-off.

Note: You must move your bowels every day during a cleanse! Latent pathogens, like viruses or bacterias, may get dislodged. If they sit in your colon, they can release back into your bloodstream and cause illness. You must move them out! Enemas may be necessary if you are not moving on your own. Consider colonics as well.

Other Considerations to Improve Gut Health

Not everybody needs supplements. It is trial and error to figure out what works best for you. Listen to your body. Eliminate the violation first.

Microbiome Gut Flora, Prebiotics & Probiotics

Your microbiome is designed to protect you. I highly recommend testing your gut microbiome if you have long term digestion issues. Your gut health can get thrown off by medication, illness, and just everyday stress. Even taking too much of a good probiotic can create bloating. The right balance is important.

Prebiotics are health building. They are present in fiber rich foods such as vegetables, fruits, and non-GMO whole grains. They actually serve as food for the good bacteria and probiotics. Besides enhancing the absorption of essential minerals, they can help prevent constipation and diarrhea. The most common prebiotic supplements come from Jerusalem artichokes and chicory.

Probiotics are present in any food that is cultured or fermented. If you **eat fermented foods** as part of your weekly habit, you usually do not need a probiotic. I frequently add a tablespoon of sauerkraut to my meals. Only once in a while, I will take a probiotic if I catch a bug to quickly change the bacteria in the colon.

Here is a list of foods that are naturally rich in probiotics:

- Sauerkraut
- Kefir
- Yogurt (without sugar)
- Kimchi
- Cottage cheese
- Tofu
- Tempeh
- Homemade sourdough bread
- Buttermilk
- Miso
- Natto
- Raw vinegars
- Raw cheese
- Wine (small amounts)

**Note: If you have bacterial yeast overgrowth or fungus, fermented foods may not agree with you until those are cleared up.

Digestive Enzymes

Some experts consider enzymes *the fountain of youth*. They are the workhorse of the digestive system. Nothing works right without enzymes. They are needed for every chemical reaction in the human body. If you do not have sufficient enzymes, your food does not break down properly, and the nutrients are not assimilated enough. Enzymes are used to build up just about everything from bone to the elasticity in our skin.

We also need enough vitamins and trace minerals to help as cofactors to be efficient. Most of the B vitamins are coenzymes. Some doctors suggest that a deficiency of vitamin B1 thiamine has a great impact on the efficiency of the enzymes. You see, vitamins do not work without enzymes, and enzymes do not work without minerals. This is why we like food-based vitamins and plant based minerals, because they have the enzymes to help utilize them. Synthetic vitamins do not have the enzymes.

Raw vs. Cooked

Foods have the highest enzyme activity level if they are fresh, local, fermented, cultured, and raw. Long shelf life foods, pasteurized, processed, packaged, and cooked foods are enzyme depleted.

You can deplete your enzyme reserves every time you eat a meal with no enzymes. If this is all you eat, your pancreas and stomach have to use your reserve enzymes in order to perform digestion. This puts stress on the organs. Enzymes are further inhibited when your Ph is off. Some medication can also block them.

If you eat mostly cooked foods, you likely need supplementation. A good basic supplement that has protease for protein, lipase for fat, and amylase for carbohydrates is a good start. There are others for specific conditions like lactose intolerance and gluten sensitivity. Gluten is a protein, so protease is likely to help break that down.

PH Acid Alkaline Balance

Keeping your Ph in balance keeps you in balance. Excess either way causes symptoms physically and emotionally. Nervous system issues develop from both acid or alkaline conditions, as well as anxiety and a host of other problems. Your body uses its mineral reserves trying to keep your Ph in order, then you end up deficient.

World famous nutritionist Paavo Airola believes that acidosis is the basic cause of all disease. FYI: Cancer grows in an acidic environment.

The more acidic we get, there is less bioelectric potential in the cells and life force. Raw foods like salads can help restore the bioelectric potential to the cells.

More people are too acidic than too alkaline. It is harder to get too alkaline, but it happens frequently to vegans that do not consume dairy and animal foods. Alcohol, white processed, soda, coffee, and excess flesh foods and fat are highly acidic.

This is an extremely brief overview, but if you do not have a general feeling of vitality and clarity, check your Ph. Most pharmacy's sell test strips. Check once in a while to see if you are in the normal range.

HCL Hydrochloric Acid Betaine

When you think of heartburn, you think you have too much acid. In fact, it is often the opposite. We don't have enough, or it is in the wrong place. Chronic use of antacids and acid blocking drugs create long term problems. Two great resources on this topic are *Why Stomach Acid Is Good For You* by Jonathan Wright and Elizabeth Lipski's *Digestive Wellness* [2.2], which has a great guide to supplementation.

Often when patients are supported with HCL betaine, plus pepsin, digestive enzymes, nourishment, and stress management, their stomach issues resolve.

Note: Please get advice from a professional and never stop taking medication without consulting your doctor.

Bile Salts

Bile Salts emulsify the fats in our diet and make calcium and iron more absorbable. People that have had their gallbladder removed do not concentrate bile acids. If you have gallbladder or liver issues, you can benefit from taking bile salts.

If you have had your gallbladder removed, have liver disease, or fail to absorb fats, consider taking bile salts with your food. If I had no gallbladder, I would take bile salts and lipase – the fat enzyme – to help digest and absorb fat.

Inflammation

- Where to Start? Try the Elimination Diet

An elimination diet is a way to test yourself for food sensitivities. You can be reacting to healthy foods and not know it. For example, many people get joint pain from nightshades like potatoes or tomatoes. You only know if you eliminate them for three weeks and see if your arthritis improves. Some people are highly sensitive to lectins.

The big triggers to experiment with first are: gluten, wheat, dairy, and eggs. Others are nightshades, soy, tree nuts, legumes, citrus, corn, peanuts, legumes, shellfish, and non-organic meats. Yes, also alcohol, sugar and fake sugar.

A nutritionist recommends eliminating all the triggers for two weeks, and then reintroducing one at a time to see if you react. You would be eating primarily clean protein, vegetables, some fruits, and good fats.

Sometimes when you are sensitive to a certain food, if you only consume it once in four days, you can avoid reacting. Some people only have an issue when they eat a food they are sensitive to for two or three days in a row. Here are some gut healing protocols to try:

- Wahl Protocol
- The Gaps Diet
- Whole 30
- Fodmap Diet

They are all a bit different but experimenting with different approaches is a great way to get to know yourself. And they can all help you with food sensitivities.

Fasting Feeds the Spirit Too

Fasting is not a new concept, we have heard about it since biblical times. It is extremely beneficial to give your digestion a break from constantly digesting food. When you graze all day, you are using and losing precious enzymes, and keeping your glycemic index elevated.

Bonus: When you give your digestion a break, you also help normalize insulin, promote cellular regeneration, minimize cravings and burn fat!

Intermittent fasting is popular now and studies show it is so beneficial for repairing the gut and giving you energy.

Start slow. Basically you are choosing a window of time to eat within; 6-8 hours is a very doable start window. So that would be two good meals a day and a good gap in the middle. The idea is that your digestion rests for 16 to 18 hours around the window and repairs.

You have to experiment and see what works for you. Dr. Berg[2.3] and Dr. Mercola [2.4] have created great videos that outline how and why to try intermittent fasting in greater detail.

Longterm: One Liquid Day a Month or Week

This step changed my health more than any other. A liquid day is not a detox, it is a cleanse; but it will get you used to the process of fasting. This will prepare you for when you are ready for a deeper systemic detox cleansing.

Start slowly beginning with one liquid day a month, and see how you feel a day or two after this day. You should have more energy. This is because you gave your body a break from digesting food and conserved energy.

When you are not using energy digesting food, then your body can heal what it needs to. I am not talking about just water and lemon, I am talking about just liquids, nourishing liquids.

This makes it easier as a first try because you will not be hungry. That means soups, smoothies, broths, and no snacking in between. I am big on making broths from grass fed bones as a base for puree soups, but if that is not for you, simply use vegetable broth.

The more you give your digestion rest and repair time, the more energy you will have.

Best Healing Food for the Gut

The best gut benefits on liquid days come from sipping homemade broth elixirs, or using them for the base of a puree soup. Watch my video on how to make delicious beef bone broth! It is available on my website (holisticwellnessplus.com)[2.5] as well as on my YouTube Channel (Holistic Wellness Plus with Michelle Corey)[2.6].

Supporting Your Detox Systems

Recall that your Lymphatic and Circulatory Systems are important for detoxification.

Encouraging Your Lymphatic System

The lymphatic system maintains fluid balance and can get congested with toxins. Below are ways to help create flow in your lymphatic system and release clogged toxins from your body.

- Some suggest jumping on a trampoline every morning or performing 10 jumping jacks to get the system going.
- Dry brushing opens the pores and encourages lymphatic drainage. Check with a doctor if you have a skin condition. Always brush towards the heart.
- Exercise or movement in any form is key. Even if you cannot walk, move your foot or hand in circles. Providing you are mobile, move your arms when walking.
- Alternative treatments like hot and cold showers stimulate the lymphatics.
- Infrared Saunas are another good option, and heal deep into the body.
- Salt or mud baths release toxins.
- Massages and special lymph drainage massage help release the toxins that are not moving.
- Eat plenty of fruits and vegetables.
- Five to ten minutes of breathwork daily promote movement.
- Drink clean water. Be sure it doesn't contain fluoride or chlorine.

Fostering the Circulatory System

The circulatory (cardiovascular) system's main function is to deliver oxygen to the tissues. It also works hard to remove carbon dioxide and other waste products. Below are ways to improve the function.

- Increase your physical activity.
- Maintain an ideal weight.
- Balance your sugar regulation.
- Smoking restricts blood flow.
- Eat heart healthy fruits and vegetables.

Are You Ready To Cleanse?

Start slow and listen to your body. Be sure to follow the order laid out in this chapter to prevent unwanted side effects. Before you begin, make sure your pathways are open and supported, and consider visiting a good Functional Medicine Doctor or Naturopath, especially if you are unwell.

Try to be patient, a full detox can take some time and the process never truly ends. I continue to practice a one-day liquid cleanse every week for long-term maintenance.

Step Three

Restore Body, Mind and Soul

Our Health involves all aspects of our life
Holistic Wellness is about body, mind, and
spirit – and it all works together.

To feel whole, healthy, and happy, we have to consider all aspects of our human selves. Unlocking our potential requires much more than great nutrition. When we are unbalanced emotionally and physically, we have disrupted our natural inner grace. This is what we call stress, and this is the major cause of dis-ease. Restore the physical, and you also balance your emotions, and vice versa. Inner harmony brings physical wellness.

The three factors that have the biggest impact on our wellbeing are:

- Stress
- Undernourishment
- Toxins (examples: heavy metals, fungus, chemicals, parasites, pathogens, pesticides, glyphosates, etc.)

Remove the stress and the toxins so the body can begin to heal itself. Then eat nourishing whole foods. Simple.

Food has the power to heal our bodies and minds. Food gives our body fuel and feeds our brain to do all the things we need to do. My mission started out years ago to be all about beauty and skin health. Turns out, what creates great skin also creates health on the inside.

Optimal health and beauty works two ways; from the inside out and the outside in. When one aspect is disrupted, it has an impact on our entire system.

When our bodies are full of toxins and unhealthy foods, we tend to feel unbalanced emotionally. I am sure you have heard reference to the gut and brain connection. Heal your gut, heal your body.

Likewise, when our inner harmony and feelings are distorted, our outer beauty is just a mask.

If you have a low physical and emotional state, the energy must shift. With every choice you make, consider if it will elevate you or deplete you.

Conscious eating reflects your highest state of awareness, and your need to function in this world. I do not believe in excluding any food group, but selectively choose high frequency, elevating food no matter what group.

Get to know your genes and your body; pay attention to how you respond to different foods. Basically, we should eat healthy fats, vegetables, fruits, and a clean source of protein, along with lots of clean water. Strive for very little processed food.

I strive toward food choices that are high in minerals and have a low glycemic index. Below are the habits I have been living for the majority of my life, which have served me well.

My Habits for Healthy Living

Honor your body (at least 85% of the time).

1. Only eat real whole foods. Anything in a box or package is not real food. Strive to eat fresh, and every color of the rainbow every day: red, orange, yellow, green, blue, indigo, and violet. These are also the colors of the seven main chakras, so you are nourishing your body, top to bottom.
2. Eat enough protein. Research indicates we need a minimum of one-third to one-half of our body weight in grams to maintain and encourage muscle mass. So if you weigh 100 lbs, strive for 35 to 50 grams. I try to have my protein in the first half of the day as it seems to sustain my energy throughout the day.

Vegan Protein Sources: If you are vegan, great choices are peas, legumes, quinoa, beans, lentils, flax, ancient grains, spirulina, hemp, and soy products. Please eat only non-GMO soy products. Keep in mind, if your goal is weight loss, most vegan protein choices are also higher carbohydrates. Nuts and seeds are good protein and are mostly fat, good fat. But if you consume more than a handful of nuts, it will add to Omega 6 burden of inflammation if not balanced with Omega 3's. (See below.)

Vegetarian Protein Sources: Vegetarians may add eggs, cottage cheese, and other dairy.

Omnivore / Meat-Eater Protein Sources: Meat eaters should eat clean 100% grass fed meat that is pasture raised, with full skin and fat. Eating meat without the fat results in rapid depletion of vitamin A, and we need vitamin A to assimilate protein. Consume nourishing broths made with grass fed bones for collagen synthesis. Homemade bone broths are "melted collagen." They nourish our joints and tendons, support digestive health, and give us beautiful skin.

About Animal Protein: Some of us need small amounts of animal protein to feel good. The serving should be about the size of the palm of your hand. Pay attention to how this digests. If it seems difficult, you may be low in HCL or enzymes, or you are mixing the protein with too many other foods. It is best to eat protein earlier in the day, either on its own or with vegetables.

3. Eat enough good fat. Good fats cannot be emphasized enough. Enjoy olive oil, avocado oil, gee, butter, coconut oil, flax oil.

4. Combine good fat and small amounts of clean protein at every meal to balance your sugar regulation. The fat and protein help to lower the glycemic index. When it is just carbohydrates, your sugar spikes.

5. For optimum benefits, grains, nuts, and seeds should be sprouted, soaked and fermented according to their intended purpose.

6. Add fermented foods for natural prebiotics and probiotics, such as kefir, yogurt without added sugar, sauerkraut, natural pickles, and kombucha.

7. Make sure part of your daily diet is raw whole fruits or vegetables to populate enzymes. This helps build your reserve enzymes. Chewing your food really well also stimulates enzymes.

8. Do not eat between meals. Grazing keeps your glycemic index high. When it is constantly high, it is harder to balance your metabolism.

9. Eat high-mineral salts like celtic sea salt or himalayan sea salt. This is a perfect way to get the minerals we need. These salts are more valuable than the typical table salt with added iodine, which is depleted of minerals.

10. Add high fiber foods to promote digestive health, reduce cholesterol, and minimize the glycemic response. These feed the micro bacteria in your gut. Try to get the fiber from vegetables rather than grains as the gluten in grains can be disruptive to the gut and spike the glycemic index.

    If you can handle lectins, consider lentils, black beans, pinto beans, and peas. Most vegetables add fiber too, like broccoli and green beans. Raspberries are a great source too! Trial and error is in order here as gut conditions like SIBO can react to fiber. So always consult a professional if you have issues.

11. Add sea vegetables like kombu, nori, sea kelp, and miso soup for micro minerals and natural iodine. Your thyroid will thank you.

12. Increase oxygen through exercise, walking and breathwork. This will increase your energy. If you are physically impaired, you can sit and deep breathe or use different techniques such as box breathing.
13. Reduce stress! - You can have the best nutrition, but if you are constantly stressed, something will give. Fortunately there are many pathways to relieving stress. Breathwork, meditation, therapy, holistic treatments like massage, reflexology or biofeedback can all be used to shift your energy. Try different modalities to see what works for you. Walk in the woods, get fresh air and sunshine. Healing the gut can also calm anxiety.
14. Water, water, hydrate! Clean water = clean body! It is suggested to consume about half your bodyweight in ounces every day. If you weigh 100 lbs, then 50 ounces is about right. I try to hydrate in the morning, it seems to help my energy levels all day. Filter water to eliminate chlorine, fluoride and other toxins.
15. Strive for quality sleep. If you follow the suggestions above, your sleep should be restorative. Often if your sugar regulation is reactive, and the gut is impaired, sleep can be disturbed. If you struggle with finding restful sleep, refer to Chapter 2 and consider a cleanse. Parasites will disturb your sleep.

Reminder:

- Reduce or eliminate alcohol.
- Reduce and eliminate sugar and processed foods.
- Reduce high Omega 6 foods, especially seed oils.
- Reduce stress.
- Be mindful of toxins.
- AVOID: GMO grains, soy, dairy, legumes, corn, or any other fake foods.

Aging

Our cellular turnover rate slows as we grow older. When the speed of cell damage exceeds the process of cell repair, we age. I strive to maximize the ability to repair in order to slow the aging process.

Overview

What contributes to cell damage?

- Oxidative stress
- Free radicals
- Elevated insulin levels
- Acidity
- Stress

Key factors for slowing aging and lowering inflammation:

- Increase oxygen / exercise
- Hydrate
- Eat real, nutrient dense, whole foods
- Eat antioxidant foods
- Have a healthy mental outlook
- Get enough sleep
- Avoid pollutants
- Master your stress
- Correct sugar regulation while you can

The bottom line: Keep your glycemic index low, increase antioxidants, reduce stress, calm your mind, forgive, and breathe.

Anti-Aging Nutrients

The #1 skin vitamin is vitamin A Retinol. The only way to get this through diet is from an animal source. I understand the controversy about this, especially in the spiritual community. However, in my practice, let me say the sickest people I have seen have been long term vegetarians.

Old fashioned bones and collagen broth is your natural way to heal your gut and reduce inflammation. This is why I love homemade broth elixirs to either sip or use as a base to make pureed soups with lots of vegetables.

Bone broth is extremely rich in vitamins, minerals, collagen, and amino acids. You can get the muscle building amino acids and the gut does not have to break it down! Not all broth is created equal. It needs to simmer for 22 hours minimum to extract all the goodness and minerals. This process makes it rich in collagen, and has been shown to help heal leaky gut when used as a sipping broth.

Collagen is a structural protein, made up of amino acids. It is essential for slowing physical signs of aging. This is the substance that keeps your skin looking firm, plump, and youthful. Collagen production decreases as we age. When we don't have enough collagen, our skin begins to wrinkle or Sag. It is also important in the prevention and/or treatment of osteoarthritis and joint pain. In addition to consuming collagen in foods like bone broth, vitamin C may help to boost your natural collagen production.

EFA (essential fatty acid) means it is essential to your body. We need them to run efficiently. Some good choices are flax, fatty fish, or nuts. Too much Omega 6 creates inflammation and has to be balanced with Omega 3. What our body needs is a 4 to 1 ratio. Most of us do not have enough Omega 3 EFA.

Note: Keep in mind that we take on the energy of what we eat. So purchase grass fed only, from a source you know cares for the animal. You eat what they eat. If you eat meat and fish, it should be grass fed, pastured, or wild. Pasture raised fosters calm, happy energy. Mass produced caged cows and chickens must be angry and frustrated. So yes, buy happy eggs!

Mineral-Rich Choices

I've mentioned that enzymes are key. They are considered the fountain of youth by some. Amino Acids are also necessary building blocks for muscle. However, it can really be said that every nutrient is important to your overall health. Everything works together. High minerals are quite vital to your wellbeing. **Vitamins do not work without enzymes, and enzymes do not work without minerals.**

Minerals are needed for the body to run efficiently. They play various roles in metabolism and body functions. Our soils used to be more mineralized, but have since been depleted. So you may need a multi-mineral supplement if you are not nourishing yourself with some of the important ones below. I will list the highest quality food sources, but this is by no means a complete list. Many other foods have smaller amounts. Variety is always best.

- **Calcium** builds bones and teeth, activates enzymes throughout the body, and helps to regulate blood pressure. (Sources: most greens, especially spinach and collards, yogurt, kale, tofu, dairy)
- **Magnesium** also builds bones and teeth. And it helps relax nerves and muscles and keep your blood circulating smoothly. (Sources: green vegetables, spinach, swiss chard, pumpkin seeds, green beans, flaxseeds, salmon, black beans)
- **Phosphorus** is used to build healthy bones, make new cells, and create energy. Note: You may need to limit your intake if you have kidney disease. (Sources: pumpkin seeds, nuts, quinoa, beans, seafood)
- **Chloride** helps regulate the amount of fluids and nutrients going in and out of cells, stimulates stomach acid, and maintains PH levels. It facilitates the important flow of oxygen and carbon dioxide within cells. (Sources: seaweed, tomatoes, lettuce, olives, celery)
- **Potassium** helps maintain calcium levels and lowers risk of high blood pressure. It balances fluids to maintain the proper electrolyte and acid base balance in your body. (Sources: swiss chard, spinach, winter squash,

beets, brussel sprouts, carrots, cantaloupe, tomatoes, broccoli, celery)

- **Sodium** balances fluids in the body, helps send nerve impulses, and helps make muscles contract. It is necessary for normal cell function. Though, excess is linked to adverse health outcomes. As with many things, a healthy balance is essential. (Sources: Choose natural salts like celtic sea or pink himalayan.)

The following are trace minerals.[3.6] Though we need lesser amounts, they are no less important.

- **Chromium** helps maintain normal blood sugar levels and insulin levels. (Sources: onions, romaine lettuce)
- **Copper** assists with metabolizing fuel, making red blood cells, regulating neurotransmitters, and mopping up free radicals. (Sources: calf's liver, sesame seeds, crimini mushrooms, walnuts, sunflower seeds, potatoes)
- **Iron** enhances oxygen distribution in the body. It is essential for activating certain enzymes and for making amino acids, collagen, neurotransmitters, and hormones. (Sources: Beef, shellfish, molasses, beets, spinach, liver, sardines, soybeans, pumpkin seeds.)
- **Manganese** protects the cells from free radical damage and helps metabolize amino acids, cholesterol and carbohydrates. (Sources: romaine lettuce, cinnamon, pineapple, spinach, turmeric, collard greens, raspberries, oats.)
- **Iodine** helps ensure proper thyroid functioning. (Sources: sea vegetables, yogurt, eggs, strawberries, cheese)
- **Selenium** greatly promotes the body's antioxidant potential, and helps induce DNA repair. It also helps assist the thyroid. (Sources: crimini mushrooms,

shitake, shrimp, salmon, tuna, calf's liver, brown rice, eggs, grass beef, sunflower seeds)

- **Zinc** helps maintain your immune system. It has antioxidant properties, assists in wound healing, bone formation, and neurological symptoms. Studies suggest it may even delay the progression of age-related macular degeneration.[3.1] (Sources: legumes, shellfish, meat, seeds, nuts, dairy, eggs, dark chocolate)
- **Molybdenum** activates several enzymes that break down toxins and prevents the buildup of harmful sulfites in the body. (Sources: lima beans, black-eyed peas, lentils, peas, almonds, cashews)

Remember: Minerals activate enzymes, and enzymes metabolize vitamins. Without minerals, the essential processes for good health and vitality begin to stall.

Restoring Habits & Lifestyle

Over time, good daily habits add up to better health.

Set the tone for the day right from the start. Take ten minutes to meditate, pray, and connect. This feeling can make a difference for at least half the day.

Sunlight nourishes. Do not underestimate fresh air and sunshine. Getting sunshine on your skin for 20 minutes each day not only stimulates Vitamin D levels, it elevates our moods. There are many studies showing people who work outside, even with poor nutrition, have better immune systems than those who work indoors, even those with impeccable nutrition.

Eat real food. Let me say there is no one specific diet that is right for all of us. We are all individuals and different foods can balance or unbalance your constitution. One thing that we do all have in common, however, is the need for pure, whole foods. Real food is medicine. One of the basic laws of life is to eat our food whole, organic, and in their natural raw state. Any food that is denatured and deficient in nutrients is considered a negative nutrient. Cooking meals from scratch is best. Processed foods also carry a lowered vibration.

Consider your environment. Eating with nature with consideration of the seasons in your location is known to enhance health, according to Westin Price.[3.2] Location is important. There is a difference in what your body needs living in a desert climate compared to a snowy or seaside location. It cannot be the same.

Choose organic. Also, keep in mind, the body is not always able to process genetically modified foods. Organic foods have the most minerals, and a high- mineral body has a high frequency. Not everyone can afford everything organic, so pick and choose what is important. Check the Environmental Working Group (EWG)[3.3] site to see what they call 'The dirty dozen'. There are some fruits and vegetables that are known to be treated with the highest concentration of pesticides. Strawberries are #1, followed by spinach.

Wash everything. Thoroughly soak and wash all produce, including organic, to rid all unwanted bacteria, pathogens and pesticides.

Give yourself a little break. We do not need perfection, but we can strive for the 85/15 rule. This includes everything in our lives and not just food. If you are eating foods that do not benefit the body, then just have a small quantity.

Invisible Ingredients For Restoring Good Health

There are invisible aspects in the way we nourish our bodies which may restore good health more effectively than those which we can measure. Positive thoughts and good energy boost your energetic frequency.

Food made with *love* has the highest frequency of all! Inferior food made with love will have a higher frequency than organic food made in anger. They nourish deeper parts of ourselves. For this reason, the energy and intention put into preparing our foods should also be considered. Nourish body, health, and spirit.

What To Remember

It is not just what you eat, but HOW you eat, and when you eat. The best diet in the world won't help you if you are not digesting the food properly. Relax when you eat. You must be able to break down the food, absorb the nutrients, carry it through the intestinal lining into the bloodstream, and assimilate the nutrients into the cells while the waste is carried to the detox organs.

If the gut is inflamed, right from the start, there is malabsorption, and then we don't assimilate the nutrients. For guidance, refer back to Chapter 2 on the gut, cleansing, and bone broth. Reduce omega 6's.

Step Four

Elevate
Keep Your Energy Flowing!
Stuck Energy Fosters Dis-ease.

You have eliminated the violations to body and
soul, and added nourishment. Now, release stored
emotions, and instill high frequency daily habits.
This is the way to feel calm, whole, and happy.

Release Stored Trauma and Elevate Your Frequency

Now that you have reduced your toxic load and restored your nourishment, there is another critical factor to feeling whole that needs to be addressed. Not only do we need to detox our physical bodies but also our emotional toxins. Awareness that this is a piece of our healing is the first step. This is often the root cause of symptoms and conditions and may be the most important missing step.

This step is two-fold. First release the toxic stuck emotions that create a density in your body, then elevate your vibrational frequency

Why is this important? Dr. Richard Gerber of Vibrational Medicine [4.1] says it's because we are multidimensional beings of energy and light, whose physical bodies are but a single component of a larger dynamic system. Our bodies are continuously influenced by higher energy dimensions of reality. We don't just thrive on oxygen, glucose and chemical nutrients, but also on high vibrational energies. If we assist our physical body to elevate with the frequencies, we have a better chance to heal and stay balanced.

Your Subtle Organizing Energy Fields (SOEFs) are impacted by unresolved stored emotions from past traumas and ancestral patterns. They need to be noticed and released in order to establish optimal health. Just noticing you have a pattern that repeats itself, often dissolves some of its holding power.

Pain and dis-ease are designed to bring our attention to what might be trying to heal. Your body talks to you if you can just listen.

Visualize – breathe into the pain – release. These types of imprints can be held anywhere in the body from your muscle or nerves to bone and blood. Have you wondered why you have had that certain pain for 20 years despite the fact that there is no physical reason for it? It is a held emotion usually from a trauma.

There are at least a dozen modalities that will help to release the unresolved stuck energy. They all help to downregulate your nervous system. When you are not in a hyper-reactive state, you are opening your mind to new possibilities, and this helps you recognize limiting patterns. We can repeat patterns for decades until we become aware.

As a practitioner, I have had the blessing to meet many gifted healers and through them have been introduced to modalities that helped me become aware of my own patterns. There is an expression that "there is no cure outside of you." The body is intelligent and has the capacity to heal. Mind-body healers believe that, while invisible, energy has the greatest ability to heal the body.

Mind-Body Healing Modalities

In my quest to evolve, over the years, I have personally experienced all of the modalities listed below. They each have great success in releasing stuck emotional imprints. Be conscious of stagnant energy and move it anyway you can. Find one or two modalities that you are drawn to and be consistent. (Note: Release the imprint and move on. Rethinking about it can bring it back in. Let it go.)

- **Somatic Therapy** is one of the therapies I love the most for releasing negative patterns. It seems to get to the heart of the issue quickly. The goal is to help you notice the physical responses brought up by traumatic memories. A good practitioner will get to the trauma that initiated the now trapped negative thought pattern, and once released, that pattern is in the past. It is designed to help heal you on a cellular level.

- **Exercise and Breathwork** are equally important in my opinion. Both have been proven to have great benefits for moving the chi (vital life force energy). Breathwork is the most underrated health benefit to increase your oxygen. Deeply breathe unpolluted air. Listening to your breath for a few minutes is a great way to start. Just close your mouth and breathe quietly for two minutes, bringing your attention to the sound of your breath. Breath can be the mind's natural tranquilizer. To enhance the benefits, get moving! At the very least, walk, stretch, and use your own hands to move the energy.

- **Meditation** on a regular basis is critical to changing your nervous system and releasing stress. It is a practice that helps you be in the present moment and enables you to switch from worry to balance. When you release stress, the body can begin to heal itself. Meditation is a powerful tool and it is free. *Guided journeys* are easy to plug into. They bring you out from a beta state into alpha and theta. The goal is to clear and calm the mind. Find someone who's voice you like to listen to. I record mine right on my phone and start the day with a short journey. It sets the tone for a better day.

- **Biofeedback** is intended to help you learn more about how your body works. It is a mind-body technique that can improve your health greatly as it corrects existing imbalances.

- **Changing perception** of negative mind chatter. When you think a thought, that thought starts down a path.

Our thoughts produce magnetic wave forms. Become aware of where you give your energy. Why would you give your energy to wasteful thoughts when you can give it to useful creativity? Dr. Joe Dispenza[4.2] shares YouTube videos on reprogramming negative minds. Invest your thoughts in what you want to create. Also, be mindful that other people's energy fields affect us, and our fields affect them.

- **Prayer** helps change our focus and connects us to God. As you speak a prayer, it becomes a vibrational pathway that serves as an energetic bridge to connect you to the divine consciousness.

- **Light medicine** is the science of connecting light with spirit for health and longevity. This will be part of our future healing modalities. Take in sunshine vitamins right at dawn. This way you avoid the more harmful rays. For more on light healthing, refer to *LIGHT MEDICINE: A New Paradigm — The Science of Light, Spirit, and Longevity* by Ana Maria Mihalcea M.D. PhD.[4.3]

- **Energy medicine** of all kinds – like **Reiki** and **Qigong** – moves stagnant energy. These are ancient practices that balance the body and spirit. Donna Eden[4.4] has many exercises for daily self-care using energy movements.

- **EFT Tapping Technique** – You are able to change emotions, or fears, from a higher to lower state using acupressure points. Each tapping session lessens the intensity of the emotion by rewiring the brain.

- **Tap into your heart** - You can simply touch your heart and take a few breaths to calm your mind chatter. The body has a heart field. It is an electromagnetic field produced through the heart that can be detected several feet from the individual. There is much to learn about the heart and brain magnetic fields. According to the Heart Math Institute, the magnetic heart field has a much greater influence on us than the brain.[4,5] Perhaps because the heart receives information from others long before it is perceived by the brain.

- **Yoga** is an ancient system integrating physical, mental, and spiritual practices. It creates balance and strength. If your body feels stiff and inflexible when you begin, the cause can be a combination of tight muscles and repressed emotions. The emotions we hold back can, over time, manifest as physical stress, pain, and tension. A good yoga practice can uncover stored emotions, bring them to the surface, and lead to emotional release.

- **Acupuncture** is a TCM practice that can stimulate different body systems to trigger a healing response. Needles placed in a specific sequence can restore the flow of blocked energy and rebalance the chakras.

- **Chiropractic adjustments** do not have to be intrusive at all. Keeping the spine aligned is a beautiful way to support the nervous system and circulation. It is beneficial to your whole body and encourages the body's natural ability to heal itself. It should be part of your self care maintenance.

- **Cranial Sacral Therapy** is a non-invasive alternative medicine technique that uses gentle touch to release restrictions in the craniosacral system to improve the functioning of the central nervous system.

- **Tai Chi, Jiu Jitsu, or any focused martial art** can act as a meditation in motion. They are especially great for balancing the mind and becoming more grounded in the present.

- **Ho'oponopono** is a Hawaiian healing prayer that unlocks your ability to heal yourself and others by clearing your limited beliefs. It is an ancient spiritual practice of forgiveness that helps to 'make things right' and has many miraculous stories. Dr. Joe Vitale is a good source to start.[4.6]

- **Sound Healing** has a great impact on our cells. We are electrical. Sing, chant, pray, hum. Create your own sounds. Listen to music that moves your soul and opens your heart.

- **Color Therapy** strengthens the aura and physical health. When a chakra is weak, surrounding yourself with the supporting color strengthens the part of the body associated with that chakra. For example, if your confidence is low, then yellow would help the solar plexus.

More on Chakras

A chakra is a spinning vortex of energy. While most people cannot see chakras, they can be sensed through intuition. When the chakras are not functioning well, there can be a dysfunction in the coordinating body areas. These are the corresponding colors, location, and physical connections associated with our seven main body chakras.

Root chakra - RED - is located in the base of the spine. Responsible for our survival and safety, and grounding. The root chakra carries your right to be here and have what you need in this lifetime. It is related to the sciatic nerve, large intestine, legs, feet, adrenals, and teeth. Gemstones to help: ruby, bloodstone, and garnet.

Sacral chakra - ORANGE - is located in the lower abdomen, genitals, and womb. It is responsible for desire, pleasure, creativity, procreation, and sexuality. It is related to the ovaries, testicles, bladder, kidneys, and lower back. Gemstones to help: carnelian, coral, and moonstone.

Solar Plexus chakra - YELLOW - is located in the navel area. It is responsible for will, power, assertiveness, and joy. It is related to the whole digestive system, stomach, pancreas, and adrenals. Gemstones to help: amber, topaz, and yellow citrine.

Heart chakra - GREEN - is located in the mid-chest region. It is responsible for compassion, love, empathy, and relationships. It is related to the thymus, immune system, lungs, pericardium, heart, arms, and hands. Gemstones to help: emerald, jade, rose quartz, and tourmaline.

Throat chakra - BLUE - is located in the throat. It is responsible for speaking your truth, communication, hearing, and creativity. It is related to the thyroid, parathyroid, neck, shoulders, arms, and hands. Gemstones to help: turquoise, aquamarine, and celestite.

Brow chakra - INDIGO - is located between the eyebrows. It is responsible for vision, intuition, headaches, and nightmares.

It is related to the eyes and pineal gland. Gemstones that help: star sapphire, quartz, lapis lazuli.

Crown chakra - VIOLET - is located at the top of the head. It is responsible for thought, understanding, awareness, and intelligence. It is related to the pituitary, central nervous system, and cerebral cortex. Gemstones that help: amethyst, diamonds.

Reaching Optimum Frequency

How do we help ourselves shift up and bring ourselves to our optimum frequency? What is the benefit?

When you elevate your vibratory rate, it increases your ability to cope with others' emotions and energy fields without absorbing their negativity. The energetic influences of the optimum frequency also keeps us physically well.

The health of our physical body is dependent on cellular voltage. We actually have a Hertz measurement. A healthy human runs about 68 MHz. Optimal cellular voltage is essential to help our cells properly communicate and also keep our energy flowing. The suggestions below have an elevated effect on the Subtle Organizing Energy Fields (SOEFs): They will increase your vibrational frequency and rejuvenate your body.

- Every thought has a frequency; every thought produces a chemical. First, **speak your truth**. live your passion, and your voltage goes up! This is how your light shines through to outer beauty.
- Deliberately **change your perception** of how you see things. Being a victim and staying a victim keeps you in a low frequency.
- **Gratitude for 20 minutes** a day strengthens the immune system. After just 10 minutes of focused gratitude, the body begins to release a chemical called immunoglobulin A.
- Can we change our physical condition with **visualization**, thoughts, and intention? Yes, move the energy with your mind.
- **Forgive**, especially yourself. "I forgive myself for all my errors."
- **Solfeggio music** has a frequency of 528 Hertz. These powerful healing tones bring balance in our body and in our lives. It is known to have the ability to offer deep healing and repair the biological body- namely the DNA. It soothes your general wellbeing as it brings a state of deep relaxation. It is known to assist in anxiety, sleep, and stress. Try tuning forks for sound healing.
- **Wear natural fabrics**, especially if you are not well. Fabric has an energetic frequency that affects our own

vibrational frequency. Cotton and linen breathe and soothe the body.

- **Homeopathic remedies** carry a frequency. The main theory behind homeopathic remedies is "like cures like" using highly diluted formulas. Cell Salts contain nature's 12 healing mineral compounds that are necessary for cellular energy. These 12 cell salts come in a combination of 12 and are necessary for the fluid in our cells to charge.

- **Harmonious thoughts.** Yes, elevated thoughts elevate you! Who do you spend most of your time with? Do they make you happy? There are studies of people with illnesses that watch comedies to make them laugh and thereby cure themselves! So yes, be mindful of your own energy throughout your day, and see if situations or people elevate you or detract you from feeling good. Honor yourself first.

- **Align with positive people.** Their vibe will raise yours.

- **Highly mineralized foods** assist the body to better health because a highly mineralized body has an elevated frequency. Fresh, raw, and alive foods are the highest of frequencies. Fresh herbs have a high Mhz. Raw foods seem to have the ability to restore bioelectric potential to the cells. Sprouted foods are considered alive, so add them to your salads and smoothies. Keep in mind that we take on the energy of what we eat. Comfort foods made in a loving kitchen will carry a higher vibration than organic food made in anger.

- **Clean water, clean body.** Water carries a frequency. Dr. Emoto has a whole study with photos of water.[4.7] As he intentionally imposes emotions into the water, the resulting patterns are remarkable.

- **Clean air, clean lungs.** Breathe deep often throughout the day. Find unpolluted air near the ocean and mountains.
- **Be in nature** as much as you can. Connect with the earth's medicine.
- **Sleep hygiene.** This is your time to recover and heal. Most of your healing occurs when you sleep. Do all you can to foster good sleep habits.
- **Sunlight** is precious. The first light of the morning is especially special. Feel the power of the sun and absorb goodness everyday.
- **Essential oils** have a hertz. Diffuse them in the air or use them topically. Some of the higher frequency ones are: Rose Oil (300+MHz), Frankincense (147 MHz), Lavender (118 MHz), Sandalwood (96 MHz), and Myrrh (105 MHz).
- **Laugh** as much as possible. Studies show humor has therapeutic benefits and can induce positive physical changes in the body. Laughter may have the ability to raise the level of infection fighting antibodies in the body.
- **Flower Essence** remedies are infusions made from the flowering part of the plant. The process captures the energy imprint of the flower to be used as a healing vibration. They can be a catalyst for change at a deep emotional level.
- **Crystals** each have their own specific healing properties that can benefit your mind, body, and soul. The vibration is used to encourage specific healing from specific stones. They can be used for many purposes from boosting the immune system to healing a broken heart. Rose Quartz is known to heal the heart. If you

choose one you are drawn to, you will often find that you are needing their properties to help you.

- **Love** is the highest frequency of all! Open your heart and feel gratitude.

Your body is a battery and you are full of salt water, which conducts electricity. All your cell membranes carry a charge. Every organ and system in your body has its own electromagnetic field. Diseases are characterized by low voltage and are the result of insufficient battery power. Sick cells have a lower cellular voltage. Dis-ease is a lack of energy, or juice.

If you are unwell, you have discharged and given away more than you have received and recharged. Your cells need a certain amount of electrical charge across their membranes to regenerate themselves. We can improve our health by raising our voltage. When our voltage is high, we have sufficient fluid across our cell membranes to keep operations running smoothly and conduct greater amounts of electrical charge. Basically all of the cell processes are dependent on the cell voltage. We are electric.

When our cells have sufficient energy running through them, they fix themselves. When the flow of energy is blocked (possibly from emotions), our bodies don't have the resources necessary to repair themselves and return to a natural energy-conserving state of homeostasis. When we return to a state of higher charge, the body's natural healing intelligence directs that energy to where it's needed.

Dr. Tennant's book *Healing is Voltage* believes loss of voltage is associated with chronic disease, and this is connected to how emotions are stored in and around the body.[4.8]

Remember you are light, you are an energy being.

Step Five

Spiritual Fitness

The Human Journey

This final and most important step is about helping you reconnect with your intuition and aligning you with your God given gifts.

I truly believe when we were born, we were disconnected from the divine to start our journey of soul growth. Our childhood environment and experiences create patterns of behavior that both help us and limit us. As we move through life, the limiting patterns surface for us to become aware of them, and then it is our job to shift these in order to evolve to our full consciousness.

Basically, we are light beings that learned to mask our spiritual identity. We can find a zillion ways to distract from our own light, but at some point, your soul begins to wake up and external distractions become less important. Distractions can be anything from alcohol and drug abuse to negative habits, victimhood, or unconsciously choosing bad relationships. Honor yourself.

Denying our spirituality creates Illness and accelerates aging. According to the writings of Hanna Kroeger[5.1], there are seven spiritual causes of ill health. Spiritual congestion also contributes to congesting our physical body. Loss of chi coming through us creates blockages and ill health. When we work on ourselves spiritually, it always reflects on us physically. We have to stay true to our soul regardless of the cost. Speak your truth.

Becoming conscious is deliberate and not a weekend course. It takes discipline and is a lifestyle. We are here in this lifetime to evolve and learn the lessons we came here to learn for this lifespan's soul growth. Some call this earth school. If you understand that you agreed to learn specific lessons before you incarnated, somehow it is easier to cope with life's painful events that happen and move on. What an honor it is for our soul to have chosen this human experience in the body and mind we were given. We each have a unique vibrational soul-frequency, which enables us to serve humanity in our own special way. We must nourish our soul and expand our vibrational frequency.

What we want to do is activate dormant DNA. Your DNA activation is a process of bringing more light into your vital body and field of awareness. This, in turn, raises your vibrational frequency. You receive a literal upgrade in consciousness, which allows you to think, act, and perceive the world in a whole new way. It accelerates your learning as a soul and will assist you in being in alignment with your wholeness. These upgrades don't come without some effort on your part. You need to put the time into your spiritual practice to open yourself up to increasing your spiritual potential. It's a co-creative process.

Know that your physical cellular structure needs to be able to handle the frequency coming through when you channel. Consider taking homeopathic cell salts to increase the amplitude of vibrations in your physical body. This will heighten the voltage of your ionically charged body fluid.

We are only renting this physical-body home of ours. We have a duty to honor this vessel with the daily self care that is necessary to nourish our body and spirit.

When friends and family say, "you have changed," this is when you know you have soul growth. Say, "thank you." When we repress our feelings, we deny our soul what we came here to experience. Be true to yourself. Speak up, use your voice. Always be kind.

You know how crystals form when there is pressure? That is how you become a diamond yourself. Life's external pressures help us shed the outdated limiting pattern. Our job is to release that energy and not hold on. Your happiness is your responsibility, pay attention to what you pay attention to.

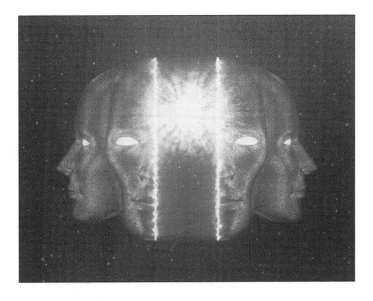

So how do we activate our sixth sense and expand our intuition?

The world's spiritual gurus teach how to activate the pineal gland, which correlates with the third eye. This gland is like the antennae receptor that receives information from universal consciousness. This area helps us to 'see beyond' what the physical eye sees. The Egyptians called it the seat of the soul. This pea-sized gland can lead you to a gateway between your physical and spiritual self.

Activating this gland will change your view on life. When it is well developed, it brings emotional and physical well-being.

Working with the Third Eye chakra and Crown Chakra together will stimulate the pineal gland. Not only does this gland help you connect to universal consciousness, it plays a vital role in maintaining your holistic health and vibrancy. This important rice-sized gland helps regulate sleep patterns, as it is responsible for the production of melatonin which regulates circadian rhythm.

The gland has been a source of interest and intrigue for mystics and healers for thousands of years. Some mystics believe calcification of this gland is caused by a toxic accumulation of fluoride, which leads to the formation of phosphate crystals and prevents the activation of the gland. Yet others say they have had an abundance of fluoride in their lives, through tap water, and have not had a negative effect. See Chapter 2 for cleansing and detoxing information which may be applied to reducing fluoride accumulation.

How do we activate the pineal gland?

A spiritual guru once told me that while you can prepare for it, "It does you. – You do not make it happen." We all have our time, just believe it will happen at the perfect time for you. Keep in mind, channeling God source has a high frequency, and you want your physical body tuned up to handle the frequency. I have seen some individuals start channeling, and the body could not handle the frequency and did not feel well for quite a long time. Many believe that a vegan diet is the only way to activate intuition. This is not best for everyone. Some of us need little bits of clean, animal-based grounding foods, or at least nourishing broths. Know your body. A healthy body means a healthy mind and spirit. We have this human body through which a higher power can create and express itself, if we are strong and grounded.

Spiritual techniques require patience and self-discipline. The heart center, pineal and pituitary gland work together. The amount of thought, focus and intention is important here. Brian Scott[5.2] recommends working with the heart center first. Breathe into the heart chakra, fill it with light, and expand and connect to the third eye chakra. Sitting erect with a straight spine allows the energy to flow from the root chakra to the pineal. Inspiration and intuition will sustain health. It all works together. When we have more life force coming through us, we are more inspired to live our purpose.

What supports the pineal gland?

In order to prepare your pineal gland, provide the right nutrition and condition. Here are ways to support and prepare the pineal gland.

- Raw fresh organic produce helps reduce calcification.
- Introduce apple cider vinegar to your diet.
- Do not expose your eyes to blue lights (from cell phones, computers, tablets, etc.) in the evening.
- Reduce exposure to electromagnetic fields (EMFs).
- Get daily sunlight exposure, especially the first light of the day.
- Practice guided meditations that bring light to the pineal gland.
- Use breathwork, proper breathing, and proper thought.
- Set intentions and ask. Prayer is asking. Meditation is listening.
- Self care assists your spiritual practice by honoring your body and spirit. Your physical body is the temple and vessel to house your divine consciousness.
- Find your purpose; make a difference. When you align with your gifts, you are more satisfied with life. People that are aligned with purpose very seldom get sick.
- Gratitude expands us. Focus on the good. Pay attention to what you pay attention to.
- Forgiveness is imperative, especially forgiving yourself.
- clear, ground, and protect (see below).

Clear, Ground, Protect

Empaths:

Please do not attempt to work on others until you have a daily spiritual hygiene routine.

Clear

I used to think I needed time to recharge. Now I know it is time needed to discharge the energy I picked up from others. You can pick up static energy just walking through a grocery store. Learn what your base self feels like. When you are 'off', know that it is not you and find ways to release the accumulated energy. Notice how you feel when you are in a great energetic state, feeling happy and strong. This is the real you. This is your base. When you feel off, think, "who is it? what is it?" We pick up emotions and thoughts from others unknowingly. Someone can be depressed or upset and just be thinking of you and it will zap your energy. Recognize this as not yours and learn to clear it up.

Intention works. "I Release from me any energy that is not mine." Salt baths help as well. Consciously release energetic debris on a regular basis throughout the day. When I wash my hands, I consistently release accumulated energy. This helps to keep my vitality high. Getting clear helps you to be divinely directed.

Ground

Do not underestimate the need to ground; it actually strengthens your intuition and helps reduce psychic overload. You are able to hold more Chi. If you feel absent-minded often, it can mean you need to ground. We are more focused and productive humans when we ground frequently.

If you have a tendency to go out of body, try eating more foods that ground you. I have a psychic friend that will have a burger after she has a channeling group to help bring her back to earth. We don't have to just depend on food. Standing on the earth is wonderful, or visualizing roots from your feet into the ground. When we are in our head with brain chatter or simply meditating and not closing, we can become ungrounded easily. We are meant to be here, present, and bring our gifts to this world. Common signs you are in need of grounding can include being spaced out, or having difficulty making decisions. Go out in nature and be with the tree.

Protect

Again, intention here is a good start. Places like hospitals and courtrooms usually carry energy that is heavy and stressful. When walking into a situation that may affect me negatively, I visualize myself in a shimmering golden hooded-cloak, and I ask Archangel Michael to shield me. "Protect me from any energy that does not serve me." Visualize a bubble around you. Protect yourself before you make a simple phone call to someone that pulls your energy. Just notice and be kind. Choose where you give your energy wisely.

Spiritual Tools

Anytime you pick up a tool, your intuition and your ability to connect is increased. They can provide validation of your intuition. Be mindful these tools do not replace your own development.

- Prayers have a vibrational frequency to bridge you and the divine. Create your own opening and closing prayer. It is very important to close down. Gratitude and ground.
- Have fun with oracle cards! Each time you pick them up, it is a message you are ready to connect. Pray first and after. Always pray.
- Use a pendulum; it is a great way to start knowing you are a vessel.
- Spiritual Response Therapy (SRT) is a great way to know yourself.
- Breathwork can get you in the zone quickly.
- Try automatic writing on a consistent basis. Many channels have started this way. Pray before and after.
- Journaling is a way to talk to the universe and tap into the field.
- Akashic record prayers are used as a vibrational pathway that helps you connect. [Please do not be reckless. You must be mindful of opening frequencies and closing them! Thanking the universal help and closing properly is extremely important.]

Law of attraction and co-creating with the universe

This is not about wishful thinking or positive affirmations. It is a deliberate practice of aligning your thoughts, emotions, and vibration with the energy of your desire to become a conscious creator. It is based on the idea that thoughts are made from 'pure energy' and that like energy can attract like energy. Feel what you have a desire for as if it is true now, and take actions toward what you want. The universe does not know the difference – if you are actually living in the desire or feeling it to be true.

Your mind, like your body, will not attract the vibrations it needs for expansion unless it is already emitting the same vibrations that it wants to attract. When you are able to do this with your mind as a tool, you can do anything.

When we have a dream or a vision we want to happen in our lives, and then we level-up to the same frequency, the dream will manifest. This is how the law of attraction works. So it is in our best interest to always elevate our thoughts, words, and actions. Be mindful of your thoughts, always. What are we focusing on? Ask – it is like writing in the universe.

This is the most magical feeling about being human. How would you like to live in synchronicity? Small miracles can happen daily. Things manifest that you just thought about in the short past. It is the ability to create your desires with spirit. Your higher power will never leave you, and is always waiting to assist you. This inner knowing and your mind are meant to be partners to help you make decisions. You know how you get goosebumps when you know something is true? This is a reinforcement that what you stated is the truth.

As you begin to notice your dreams become reality, you will naturally rely on your imagination to produce evidence. This is your personal power.

Final Thoughts

Spirituality is a way to help you cope with life stresses. When you connect to the source, you instantly start to feel calm and more positive. I think it is because it gives you hope and faith that God knows what he is doing, and we are always being guided. It enhances positive feelings. That is what it does for me anyway.

When you ask to connect to the divine, it brings you love and light, and it will keep you walking your truth. It keeps you solid and whole. Expand your essence daily to walk in your purpose. Ask for signs that you are on the right track and help you follow your spiritual truth. Follow the energy.

Connecting to source and living in peace and contentment is your reward – and easier achieved when you are a clean vessel. Treat your body like the holy temple that it is.

Who did you agree to be before you came here? What are you offering the world? This is why you incarnated here. When we are spiritually fit, we bring our gifts and contributions to the world. When we repress our feelings, we deny our soul the full experience it came here to discover. Know you are guided and supported every step of the way.

We must trust with all our heart!
Gratitude attracts the light.

Forgive us our trespasses
as we forgive those that trespass against us.

Get clear, connected, and divinely directed.

AMEN

CITED WORKS AND ADDITIONAL REFERENCES APPENDIX 1

1.1 Wilson Disease. John Hopkins Medicine. Retrieved April 26, 2023, from hopkinsmedicine.org/health/conditions-and-diseases/wilson-disease

1.2 National Institute of Diabetes and Digestive and Kidney Disease. (2020). High Blood Pressure & Kidney Disease. niddk.nih.gov/health-information/kidney-disease/high-blood-pressure

1.3 Jayne, M. (2010). Is Salt "BAD" for you? Doctor Mary Jayne: doctormaryjayne.com/diet-nutrition/11-mercola-salt-article

1.4 Sissons, Mary. (2023). Is aspartame safe, and what are its side effects and health risks? Medical News Today: medicalnewstoday.com/articles/322266#metabolism

1.5 Arnold, L. E., Lofthouse, N., & Hurt, E. (2012). Artificial food colors and attention-deficit/hyperactivity symptoms: conclusions to dye for. Neurotherapeutics: Journal of the American Society for Experimental NeuroTherapeutics, 9(3), 599–609. https://doi.org/10.1007/s13311-012-0133-x

1.6 Nelson, Marilee. (2019). The Bizarre Truth About "Natural Flavors." Branch Basic: branchbasics.com/blogs/food/the-bizarre-truth-about-natural-flavors?pdp-test=alternate

1.7 Watson, Stephanie. (2019). Microwave Popcorn Causes Cancer: Fact or Fiction? Healthline: healthline.com/health/microwave-popcorn-cancer

1.8 Environmental Working Group. (2018). Roundup for Breakfast, Part 2: In New Tests, Weed Killer Found in All Kids' Cereals Sampled. www.ewg.org/news-insights/news-release/roundup-breakfast-part-2-new-tests-weed-killer-found-all-kids-cereals

1.9 EWG Water Search Database: www.ewg.org/tapwater

CITED WORKS AND ADDITIONAL REFERENCES APPENDIX 2

2.1 Belen, Susana. We Care Spa. (February 2007). Detox and Revitalize. Square One Publishers.

2.2 Lipsky, Elizabeth. (2011) Digestive Wellness. 4th Edition. McGraw Hill Education.

2.3 Berg, Eric. (December 2018). How To Do Intermittent Fasting Printable Guide. Dr. Berg. https://www.drberg.com/blog/how-to-do-intermittent-fasting-printable-guide

2.4 Dr. Mercola. Intermittent Fasting Infographic. https://www.mercola.com/infographics/intermittent-fasting.htm

2.5 (Website) Corey, M. (October 2020.). How to make delicious immune-boosting collagen beauty broth. Holistic Wellness Plus. https://www.holisticwellnessplus.com/blogs/health/how-to-make-delicious-immune-boosting-collagen-beauty-broth

2.6 (YouTube) Holistic Wellness Plus. (2021). How to Make Delicious Bone Broth and Boost Your Immune. YouTube. Retrieved May 15, 2023, from https://www.youtube.com/watch?v=wcsQkmG-mBc.

2.7 Gates, Donna. The Body Ecology Diet. Hay House Inc. 2011.

CITED WORKS AND ADDITIONAL REFERENCES APPENDIX 3

3.1 Nordqvist, Joseph. (April 2023). What are the health benefits of zinc? Medical News Today: https://www.medicalnewstoday.com/articles/263176

3.2 Weston A Price. (2009). Nutrition and Physical Degeneration. Price-Pottenger Nutrition Foundation, 8th edition.

3.3 EWG (2023). DIRTY DOZEN™. Environmental Working Group: https://www.ewg.org/foodnews/dirty-dozen.php

3.4 Mateljan, George. (2006). The World's Healthiest Foods. GMF Publishing. Chicago, IL.

3.5 Gundry, Steven. (2019). The Longevity Paradox: How to Die Young at a Ripe Old Age. Harper Wave. New York, New York.

3.6 Berg, Eric. (2023). Trace Minerals Are NOT Just for Hair, Nails and Skin. Web: drberg.com/blog/trace-minerals-are-not-just-for-hair-nails-and-skin

CITED WORKS AND ADDITIONAL REFERENCES APPENDIX 4

For in depth knowledge of the chakras, I recommend the book Wheels of Life by Anodea Judith, PhD

4.1 Gerber, Richard. (March, 2001). Vibrational Medicine: The #1 Handbook of Subtle-Energy Therapies. 3rd edition. Bear & Company. Vermont.

4.2 Dispenza, Joe. (n.d.). Drjoedispenza [YouTube Channel]. Retrieved July 13, 2023, from URL https://www.youtube.com/channel/UCSTTPGPS-lm0YVb4DMJ3lTA

4.3 Mihalcea, Ana Maria.(2021). LIGHT MEDICINE: A New Paradigm — The Science of Light, Spirit, and Longevity. Arthema Sophia Publishing. Yelm, WA.

4.4 Eden, Donna. (2020). Donna Eden's Daily Energy Routine [YouTube Video]. Retrieved July 13, 2023, from URL: https://www.youtube.com/watch?v=Di5Ua44iuXc

4.5 Heart Math Institute (n.d.). Science of the Heart - Exploring the Role of the Heart in Human Performance [webpage]. Retrieved July 13, 2023 from URL: https://www.heartmath.org/research/science-of-the-heart/energetic-communication

4.6 Vitale, Joe. (n.d.). Transform To Success Your Life with Ho'oponopono. [Webpage] Retrieved July 13, 2023 from URL: https://joevitalehooponopono.com/success-hooponopono

4.7 The Wellness Enterprise. (March, 2017). Dr. Masaru Emoto and Water Consciousness. [Webpage] Retrieved July 13, 2023 from URL: https://thewellnessenterprise.com/emoto/

4.8 Tennant, Jerry. (June, 2010). Healing is Voltage: The Handbook, 3rd Edition. [book]. CreateSpace Independent Publishing Platform.

CITED WORKS AND ADDITIONAL REFERENCES APPENDIX 5

5.1 Kreogher, Hanna. (January, 1997). Seven Spiritual Causes of Ill Health 1, 2nd edition. Kroeger Herb: Boulder, CO.

5.2 Scott, Brian. (2020). Guided Meditation Opening The Heart Chakra. [YouTube Video]. Retrieved July 28, 2023, from URL: https://www.youtube.com/watch?v=qLZYu83cOcU.

Additional References:

Schwarz, Jack. (1980). Human Energy Systems, 6th edition. Dutton: Boston, MA.

Burney, Diana. (September, 2010). Spiritual Clearings: Sacred Practices to Release Negative Energy and Harmonize Your Life. North Atlantic Books: Berkeley, CA.

Printed in the United States
by Baker & Taylor Publisher Services